I0154144

John Cooper

Christian Evolution

The divine process in human redemption - with an appendix on the

revision of creeds

John Cooper

Christian Evolution
The divine process in human redemption - with an appendix on the revision of creeds

ISBN/EAN: 9783337367954

Printed in Europe, USA, Canada, Australia, Japan

Cover: Foto ©Lupo / pixelio.de

More available books at **www.hansebooks.com**

CHRISTIAN EVOLUTION

OR

THE DIVINE PROCESS IN HUMAN REDEMPTION

WITH AN APPENDIX ON THE
REVISION OF CREEDS

BY

REV. JOHN COOPER,

AUTHOR OF "SCIENCE OF SPIRITUAL LIFE," "PROVINCE OF LAW," "CHRIST'S
MODE OF PRESENTING HIMSELF TO THE WORLD," "SELF-SACRIFICE," ETC.

EDINBURGH:
MACNIVEN AND WALLACE.
1884.

PREFACE.

THIS volume is intended as a supplement to the Author's previous four volumes. If Christianity is to rise in these days to her true commanding position, it will be by bringing the essential truths of the Gospel into clearer prominence. Stronger emphasis must be given to the innate greatness of free agency, the evil character of sin considered as self-worship, and the true grandeur of self-sacrifice in reclaiming the rebellious spirit of man to the loyal devotion of Christian life. The Author would fain do what lies in his power to restrain, in some degree, the declension from the Christian profession which appears to be so lamentably prevalent at present.

CONTENTS.

CHAPTER I.

THE CHRISTIAN DOCTRINE OF EVOLUTION.

CHAPTER II.

DIVINE ACTION : DIRECT AND INDIRECT.

Contents.

CHAPTER III.

RECONCILIATION.

8 *Contents.*

CHAPTER IV.

THE UNPARDONABLE SIN.

CHAPTER V.

THE ELECTION OF GRACE.

APPENDIX.

REVISION OF CREEDS.

I.

THE CHRISTIAN DOCTRINE OF EVOLUTION.

CHAPTER I.

THE CHRISTIAN DOCTRINE OF EVOLUTION.

"I am set for the defence of the gospel."—ST PAUL.

1. ELSEWHERE we have shown that a reasoned Christianity is the want of the day. Rationalism is Pilate sitting in judgment upon Christ, asking Him, what is truth? and refusing to hear His reply. The controversy between evangelical and evolutionary Christianity is already declared. By many eminent teachers in the Church, evolution is received as an infallible truth, and evangelical doctrines are held to be but corruptions of Christian myths, capable of any interpretation the teacher may choose to give them. To meet the plausible objections of such reasoners, the defenders of evangelical truth must present it in its spiritual rather than in its formal aspects. They must show that, while Christianity is not discoverable by the keenest powers of human reason, it is yet so adapted to the rational

nature of man as to fit in with every requirement of his moral and spiritual being, and is
capable of proving itself the sole power by which
reason can attain to its loftiest and noblest development. In order to steer a straight course
between scepticism on the one hand and super-
stition on the other, Christianity must be
presented as a system of truth addressed to
man as a rational being. It is too sacred a
thing to stand upon human tradition, ecclesiastical authority, or human dogmas. It is
the very light of heaven, adapted to the nature,
wants, and circumstances of man. It is a light
shining upon man direct from God, to enable
him to see himself as he really is, and to show
him the way of life. Christian devotion is not
mere feeling, nor the blind apprehension of an
unknown God. It is emotion awakened and
fed by the intelligent apprehension of the
Fatherhood of God. In His self-revelation,
God addresses man as a reasonable being.
Reason reads the character of God as it is
disclosed in the light of revealed truth. In the
perfect fellowship of heaven alone, faith gives
place to sight. The blessed spirits in glory
" know as they are known."

2. Were Christian devotion realized only in
feeling, it would not be the communion of man's

entire nature with God. It would not have
needed that Christ should come into the world ;
the rites and ceremonies of the Mosaic system
would have sufficed for all human requirements.
But Christ not only reasoned with men ; He
gave them such views of divine truth as meet
the wants of the human understanding, and fire
the heart with the purest emotions of grateful
love. The light of heaven seen by the eye of
reason is, to the believing soul, communion with
the Father through the Son, and by the Holy
Spirit with all its fellow-believers.

3. No intelligent student of Nature will question the scientific character of an enlightened
conception of the possibility of evolution in
Nature. The natural principles, powers, and
laws which operate harmoniously in. the production of results, act with unerring certainty.
In the ordinary operations of Nature and of
human life, we can logically infer the character
of the action from the motive, the effect from
the cause. The principle of heredity acts in
the production cf like from like, and the habits
are formed in accordance with the conditions of
the life derived from its ancestors. By evolution
we deduce the Cosmos from the original fire-
mist, the speciality of life from the speciality of
the bioplasm, the moral character from the

sequence of invariable laws in the individual life. But can such reasoning be applied to the coming into existence of evil, or the descent of the infinite into the finite, or the regeneration of the human soul? These are facts in the history of humanity as indisputable as the development of the Cosmos from the movements of the original fire-mist. The admission of these facts compels us to the admission of *breaks* in the order of human life, just as there are missing links in the evolution of Creation.

4. Are such breaks inconsistent with the principles, powers, and laws of human existence? Whilst they are obviously out of the order of development, are they inconsistent with the operations of law? Plainly, the origin of evil was the violation of moral law. But this violation was in accordance with the regular operations of psychological law. The descent of the infinite into the finite, again, though not brought about by the operation of law, was yet in perfect accordance with the laws of human existence. Regeneration is in no way the result of self-will in man; it is nevertheless produced in him in accordance with the laws of his moral life and nature.

5. Regeneration is a *break* in the order of sinful existence, effecting reconciliation with

God. Sin is a deviation of the finite will from perfect accord with the infinite will. It is the greatest calamity possible for the finite life. Self-will is stubborn and rebellious—a restless will, incapable of calm serenity or self-restoration. Sin necessitates the sinner's eternal suffering, from the endless conflict with the very conditions of the sinner's own well-being. Scripture teaches that sin has been permitted, not for its own sake, but in order that from it God might take occasion, through His own self-sacrifice, to show the riches of His grace by raising the repentant sinner to the highest possible condition of glory and happiness.

6. To this end God does all that is consistent with His own character to rescue the sinner from his sins. By this view of the awful mystery of sin alone are we able to justify God's ways to man. If, through atonement and regeneration, sinful man may be raised to a loftier condition of dignity and glory than would ever have been possible to him in an unfallen condition of being, we need but lightly regard this temporary errant state of shame and suffering. Through faith in Jesus we are able to display the heroism of Christian character, and to rise to the imitation of our great pattern, and to fellowship with Him.

7. Struggling to rise superior to sin through self-sacrifice, we acquire the elements and lineaments of the divine life. This view of the Gospel reveals to us a power constantly in action adapted, and adequate, to raise the sinner to the loftiest condition possible to his consciousness.

8. The peculiar and distinguishing difference of the Christian view from the purely scientific view of the universe is its manifestation of *breaks* in the divine order of Nature and of human life. In the salvation of man, for example, there is seen the operation of a power *above* Nature, and yet acting in accordance with Nature and law. Self-sacrificing love takes occasion from sin to display the profound depths of the essence of uncreated being. Through the operation of faith on the soul, God raises the repentant sinner from the abyss of sin to the loftiest ranks of the redeemed.

9. The creation of free agency involved the exertion of the highest creative power, called into action the profound and comprehensive wisdom of the Godhead, and opened new possibilities of being lying far beyond the conception of any finite existence.

10. The Incarnation was the Infinite coming down into the conditions of humanity, in order

to confront all the results of the creation of free agency.

11. The conflict involved in the death on Calvary was the highest combination of free agency and omnipotent power ever exhibited to the universe.

12. Christ's resurrection and ascension was His entering into His reign of love in light.

13. The principle of conquest in the salvation of man is the principle of self-sacrifice in the Godhead.

14. Christianity does not conform itself in its operations to the conditions of ethics, science, or philosophy. Atonement, regeneration, and sanctification are not products of the wisdom of this world. Nevertheless they are originated and act in perfect accordance with the principles of philosophy, the requirements of science, and the teachings of ethics.

15. In all God's ways towards man there are the highest displays of wisdom, yet not the wisdom of this world. But this does not imply that human wisdom is in accordance with the divine wisdom ; its principle is *self*, whilst the principle of the divine wisdom is *self-sacrifice*.

II.

DIVINE ACTION, DIRECT AND INDIRECT.

CHAPTER II.

DIVINE ACTION, DIRECT AND INDIRECT.

1. WILL is the movement of personality. In the finite personality it is the action of the moment; in the infinite personality the action is eternal. In the former, the movement is in accordance with the inclination of the moment and in the direction of the object of supreme desire. Right volition will always be in submission to the supreme will, and in harmony with the constitution of the universe; but selfish volition is in opposition to the supreme will, and in conflict with the divine ends.

2. A perfect unity of wills is possible, and its attainment presents the most sublime conception possible to the human mind. The finite will in complete oneness with the will of the infinite Father is the grandest conceivable moral ideal. To accept and co-operate with the infinite will is the noblest and most felicitous action of the finite being. It is not alone acting in accordance with the omnipotent will, but it secures for

C

the finite existence the perfection of its own well-being. It is the absolute perfection of free agency—the highest power of the finite being exercised in the grandest conceivable act. For, what nobler or more glorious purpose can be formed by any finite being than resolving to make the choice of the absolute will also its own? What higher condition of conscious existence is, for it, conceivable?

3. In this unity of wills was shown the glory of the Saviour's earthly life. His unbroken fellowship with the Father was the most conspicuous feature of even His perfect character. "Verily, verily, I say unto you, the Son can do nothing of Himself, but what he seeth the Father do; for what things soever He doeth, these also doeth the Son likewise; for the Father loveth the Son and sheweth Him all things that He Himself doeth." "I can of Mine own self do nothing; as I hear, I judge; and My judgment is just, because I do not Mine own will, but the will of My Father which hath sent Me." These are words full of as profound meaning as any the Saviour ever uttered. They are His omniscient discernment of the true fundamental principle of all well-being and all righteousness of life.

4. But a diversity of wills is also possible.

This possibility arises out of the freedom of
the will—the personal choice—the individual
responsibility. Were diversity *not* possible, there
could be no freedom of personal choice or individual responsibility. There would be no finite will
at all—nothing but despotic necessity and iron
fate. A diversity of wills is therefore an inevitable possibility. But so long as the will of the
creature is in accord with that of the Creator,
there is unity of will throughout the entire
universe—a oneness of power in all the movements of creation. Perfect harmony reigns in
all the operations of cause and effect. When,
conversely, the will of the creature trembles in
the balance, hesitates in its choice of abiding in
oneness with the supreme will, or resolves on the
attainment of the forbidden object, then there
is active disobedience to the primary law of life.
A separation, an opposition and conflict of wills,
at once arises. The supreme will and all loyal
finite wills are moving in the harmonious operations of law and power, whilst the disloyal and
disobedient will is acting for the promotion of
universal discord and conflict. The opposition
does not originate in any absolute requirement
of the will to test its freedom by an act of disobedience. Did such a requirement exist, it
would prove the impossibility of freedom. The

slightest deviation of the will of the creature from the absolute will must be wrong—wrong as to spiritual action and spiritual relationship, and disastrous in the result. There is then a violation of the first principle of perfect existence.

5. In the opposition of wills a new power comes into existence — the power of disobedience by the perversion of choice. The perfect concord of wills is broken by the action of selfishness. There is no longer conformity with the perfect will. The creature in opposition to the constituted order of the universe perverts the power of choice, disobeys the first law of life. Opposition to the supreme, all-perfect, benevolent, loving will must involve the selfish in indefinite suffering and misery.

6. For this perversion of the finite will there was not, and could not have been, any provision in the original constitution of the universe. It could not have the sanction or approval of the supreme will. If otherwise in any degree, there would not, in fact, have been any perversion of choice at all. Provision would have been made in the divine purpose for rebellion against the Creator! This would be the beginning of that conflict of forces in the universe which tends to its destruction.

7. The perversion of will, then, is the beginning of sin. Self-will is opposition to the very perfection of being, and is therefore sin in action. Two absolutely perfect wills cannot be at discord with one another. The utmost deviation of the finite from the infinite will involves, of necessity, every possible phase of selfishness, wickedness, and misery. And every deviation of the will is possible, when it allows itself to be swayed for the possession of any external object in preference to its own inward peace and perfection.

8. Selfishness is the only possible explanation of the opposition of wills. Why should any finite will deviate from the supreme will? It cannot be for any higher or more righteous end than that desired by the supreme will. It can only be for some lower and selfish end. But a selfish object, sought in opposition to eternal and infinite goodness, *must* be a bane, and not a blessing.

9. The universal sinfulness and misery of man is thus fully explained. It is impossible to gainsay the fact that man, as a rule, acts from self-will. The assertion of its personal will is the first conscious act of the human being. Why is the government of parent, master, magistrate, sovereign needful, if not because the bias to selfishness is universal in man?

10. A mixture of black with white destroys its purity; a single harsh note destroys melody. A healthy body comes under the influence of infection, and disease begins to operate. The action of disease counteracts the beneficent operation of the laws of health, and is intense just in the degree in which the abnormal principle prevails over the normal operation. There is sickness; but by the aid of medical skill the balance is restored. When the abnormal principle absolutely overcomes the normal operation, death ensues.

11. And so of the action of sin in the universe. At the creation, all wills were in unity with the supreme will. All principles, laws, and forces acted in harmony for the highest ends. Self-will intruded amidst the concourse of unselfish wills, and the fair Cosmos became a region in which the principles of conflict and destruction rule and operate.

12. This sad state of things was not brought about by any defect in the principles, laws, or forces of being, or by any operation of Nature, but solely by the introduction of the new and evil principle of self-will. All disorder, suffering, death, is but the necessary operation of self-will intruding between the supreme will and the operation of its own laws. When self-will be-

comes a factor amongst the operative forces of
the universe, there is, and must be, the introduction of disorder and destruction.

13. When the will of the creature deviates in
any degree from the will of the Creator, it becomes a disorganizing force. It is destructive,
because it is a rebellious force, working in opposition to the supreme beneficent will. Hence
spring all disorder, misery, and death.

14. Evil, then, is solely the abuse of free
agency. There can be no other factor in its production than the perversion of the free will.
Freedom is the highest possession of intelligent
existence. The bringing of it into being was
the highest act of creative energy. With reverence be it said, the Creator *assumed* to himself
the highest responsibility in calling it into existence. Thus much appears to be implied in the
Mosaic account of the creation. The writer, in
his narrative of the completion of the creative
work, tells us of the Godhead in divine council
over the creation of free agency—the production
of a being in the very image of God—a creation
containing in it the possibility of rebellion. But
the responsibility then assumed was more than
fully met in the atoning work of Christ.

15. The Godhead assumed all the responsibility of creating free agency ; and to man was

given the responsibility of exercising his freedom for good or evil. Terrible, indeed, have been the results in time, but grand and glorious will be the final outcome in eternity.

16. Was freedom of will, then, called into existence because it was the loftiest act of creative skill, and because its existence opens up the possibilities of grander and nobler conditions of life for man ? Doubtless, the selfish existence is the most degraded and unhappy condition of conscious life ; but it possesses other and loftier possibilities. There is opened to our view *the possibility of self-sacrifice even in the Godhead itself*—the most God-like manifestation of the divine being. Through the self-sacrifice of the Godhead, moreover, there was rendered possible self-sacrifice in man. And *this* affords him the means of living the divine life in time, and of ascending to the loftiest heights of glory in the eternity to come.

17. Men choose the life of self-will, and yet dream of attaining to well-being. By prayers and supplications they labour to influence the infinite will, and to turn it from its fixed course of rectitude. They groan and suffer, with the vain purpose to induce the immutable will to rescue them from the woes which come of clinging to their own self-will. But they find the

heavens above them as brass, and the earth beneath them as iron. The absolute will deviates not by a hair's breadth, while yet the Father surrenders His well-beloved Son, in awful self-sacrifice, to change the selfish will into a will of loyal devotion! In *this* is manifested the grace of God and the glory of man. The struggles of humanity to overcome self, and to rise into oneness of will with God, is the grandest training which an immortal spirit can undergo. This view of the life of probation on earth opens up to the mind a wondrous vision of the inconceivable glories to come.

18. Self-will is the perversion of the loyal will of the child of God. It is essentially evil —a rebellious and antagonistic force, to God and to all well-being. It works only for evil. To the full extent in which it interferes with the operation of the eternal laws—the principles of existence—the laws of life—it works only for destruction. Intruding between the will of the Creator and its operations, self-will is a force acting for the *overthrow* of the divine government. To the utmost extent of its operation it interferes with the ends and purposes of the divine order of the universe.

19. In no way, therefore, can self-will be approved by God. He can only condemn and

restrain its operations. As of the surging ocean, so of self-will He says, " Hitherto shalt thou come, and no further, and here shall thy proud waves be stayed." Self-will being essentially evil, working only for evil and in conflict with eternal law, *cannot* be employed by the Creator. He can only permit its movements, and He does so not for its own sake, but only in order that He may take occasion from it to work out still higher divine ends.

20. The right of acting in and from His own will is the prerogative of the supreme God alone. It is so, because God is essential perfection. This is the attribute which the Scriptures call the " glory of God "—the absolute perfection of His being, manifested in the perfection of His actions—the honour which He cannot give to another. Self-will, on the contrary, is the idol which God will not suffer to mount into His throne. The controversy between God and man solely concerns the selfish will. His high and rightful prerogative He holds for Himself alone.

21. In discussions about the divine decrees, we must guard against overlooking the distinction between the loyal co-operation of all obedient wills with the divine will, and the disloyal action of self-will for its own ends.

Herein lies the distinction between the Cosmos and this world—between sin and holiness—between health and sickness—between misery and happiness—between the decree of God and the self-will of rebellious man. The glory of God is not " in ordaining whatsoever cometh to pass," but in upholding the supremacy of His own will, and in drawing all wills into perfect unity with it. The brightness of the Father's glory is the great Physician of souls, Who, in the manifestation of the divine self-sacrifice, accomplished, in accordance with the Father's will, the most stupendous of all the works of omnipotence, in order to bring the operations of the rebel will into the loyal obedience of filial will. We must be careful to distinguish between the *direct* and the *indirect* decrees of God. God *cannot* decree evil. The self-will of the sinner, coming in between the will of God and its operations, is the sole cause of evil in the universe.

III.

RECONCILIATION.

CHAPTER III.

RECONCILIATION.

1. RECOVERY is different from, or rather is opposite to, development or evolution. Restoration to health, or to friendship, have each their respective conditions. In the one, the vital forces within the body must cooperate with the medicine administered ; in the other, the affections must lay hold of the manifestations of kindness. The reconciliation of enemies—the reclaiming of the rebellious will to loyalty—is the most difficult of all undertakings either to human or divine power.

2. Man, as a responsible being, forms part of a constituted order of existence, and stands in certain relations to God, to himself, and to the universe. He possesses powers and capacities out of which spring obligations to God, to himself, and his fellowmen. In endowing him with these powers, and placing him in their various relations, God has set him under laws—within and over him—to which he is subject.

3. Man has affections which can only find

adequate exercise when they are supremely
fixed on God. He has capacities which can
alone realize their true operation through the
dwelling in him of the Divine Spirit. He is
conscious of the world's influence upon him,
sensible of its drawing him away from God.
He is, moreover, conscious of the possession of
the power of *choice*, in regard to God and the
world. He may unite himself to God, and
refuse union with the world ; or he may prefer
union with the world, and violate his sense of
obligation to God.

4. Thus man is the subject of a threefold
consciousness. By uniting himself with the
world, and separating himself from God, he
disturbs the relations of his life, and awakens
within himself the sense of guilt—the operation of a self-condemning force—and so offends
God. All this is more or less clearly realized in
consciousness. The momentary gratification of
self-will, in its defiance of conscience, places
him in opposition to his own well-being ;
whereas an act of self-denial, in withstanding
temptation, lifts him into the realization of a
conscious power of self-enjoyment and of true
greatness.

5. But man is not created only to suffer.
Affliction and misery are abnormal to his very

nature. He can never reconcile himself to suffering. Had the Creator made man only to suffer, He would have created a being expressly to revolt vainly against his Maker. The struggle of man is to release himself from suffering. All the activities of mankind, properly understood, are but a part of this struggle. Yet of himself man cannot rise out of his suffering. The whole experience of the human race proves nothing if not this.

6. The idea of, and the desire for, justice are deeply imbedded in human nature. But are these ever realized in the actions of human life? When one man injures another, and is punished by the law, does his punishment (whatever it may be) undo the wrong he has committed? Can there, in fact, be perfect justice in the dealings of fallen men with one another? Is not this a simple impossibility? Is not every sinful act a separate injustice?

7. It may be answered that the idea of retaliation, or of punishment for crime, is deeply seated in human nature; doubtless, no nation, no community, no family, no individual, that ever lived on the face of the earth has been wholly destitute of this idea. But the question may be further pressed, does this sentiment of retaliation spring from the fallen or the unfallen

D

nature of man? Is it not grounded in selfishness, rather than in goodness? Is punishment
an act of justice? Can it be justified on any
other ground than that it is needful for the
protection of society?

8. The idea that punishment is a satisfaction
to law is a common, but very superficial, notion.
There is no law *really* just excepting the law of
God. But punishment is no satisfaction to the
law of God, and certainly not to God Himself.
The punishment, degradation, and banishment
of the sinner from God, and from his own well-
being, is an exhibition of the divine *wrath*, not
of the divine will and pleasure.

9. There is in God both the ability and the
determination to maintain every power, faculty,
and function he has brought into existence,
and to uphold these in all their actions upon the
several relations into which they may be brought;
until either those of them which are capable of
exhaustion wear themselves out, or, through a
higher power acting on them, are brought into
harmony of nature in the perfection of being.

10. Temptation is an agitation of the soul in
desire, produced by the influence of an external
object on the soul; or, it is the craving of the
spirit after a forbidden object. It endorses the
design of the tempter by complying with his
will.

11. Sin is the deliberate resolve to do the forbidden deed, and to secure the thing desired, irrespective of the teachings of duty. It is the choosing for self, not for brotherhood. The immediate consequence of sin is agitation of spirit, a darkening of the mind, a weakening of the power of resistance and of the resolution to abide by the right. The realization of the effects of sin is loss of the conviction of doing right, a sense of unworthiness, a fear of consequences, and a dread of wrath. There may be an effort to rise out of this disturbing consciousness, and a dreadful sense of inability to do it. Now, the infliction of the divine wrath is the maintenance of this condition of self-conflict. This is equity both to power and to law, and to the superintending providence of God.

12. Even in paradise man proved himself to be not superior to evil, or unchangeable in his loyalty to the divine will. Left to himself, he would never return to God. Nor could he, by any type, ceremony, or rite prefiguring deliverance, be restored to supreme love to God.

13. Man, the fallen being, can only be raised by divine grace. And this grace can be brought to bear savingly on the sinner only through his perception of a self-sacrificing act in God. Fatherly compassion—a purpose of mercy—a

gracious self-humiliation on his behalf—is needful to touch his rebellious spirit with quickening
love.

14. But self-sacrifice is not *in itself* a desirable
thing. Were it so, it would not be self-sacrifice.
Neither can it be imposed ; it must be purely
voluntary. God, in saving man through an act
of His own self-sacrifice, acts on man in perfect
accordance with his free and rational nature, so
as to draw forth his gratitude and love. The
application of this power of self-sacrifice to the
human spirit is the deepest moral principle in
Christianity. Every effort to raise man morally
on any other principle fails, and must fail.

15. Man must have something external to
himself on which he can repose. He is not self-
existent, self-sufficient, self-sustaining. Neither
is he *self-renewing.* Such a power is not in
Nature, or in law, but only in God. It lies in
God's condescending to meet sinful man upon
his own level. It is a power that must be
antagonistic to human corruption and in conflict
with human prejudice—with man's false conceptions of, and his dislike to, the divine order :
in a word, to his selfishness. And it must be in
harmony with human well-being. It must act
in accord with the true principles of man's life,
the functions of his nature, the law of his con-

stitution, the powers of his being, the constituted order of his well-being, and the true end of his existence. It must meet his craving after happiness, and harmonize the internal discord. It must *transform* him : he longs to be other than he feels himself to be. It must raise him to the conscious sense of a divine power dwelling in him. It must reconcile him to the law that condemns him to his face. Can he love the administration of a law which punishes him by the stern infliction of penalty? And this power must be reconciling in God : for He cannot justify or approve of the sinner who hates His administration, His law, or Himself. Hence the power, to be reconciling, must effect a change in man by a manifestation to him of the justice of the divine administration. The sinner will not repose in the God who manifests His displeasure toward him. Neither will he love the law that demands the infliction upon him of its severe penalties. A child well knows the difference between an angry and a loving and approving father.

16. But for the undoing of sin, or the removal of its consequences, man is powerless. He cannot readjust the disturbed relations of his existence, nor silence the accusing voice of conscience, nor remove the frown of displeasure

from the countenance of God. In all ages, in all lands, he has striven to accomplish this most desirable object. The incessant inquiry of the race is, "Who will show us the chief good?" What else is the desire of all nations, but the discovery of what may meet the deep necessities of human well-being? How earnestly and perseveringly has philosophy set itself to the task of discovering this power, and how unsuccessfully!

17. No penance, no repentance, can silence the inner accusations, or bring God back to His throne in the human heart. Even human sacrifices have not availed to remove the universal sense of guilt. The blood of bulls and of goats does not take away the consciousness of sin. Nor has self-righteousness removed the power of displeasure from the face of God. All have failed to impart a right direction to the longings of the spirit, to give a true knowledge of sin and its consequences, to awaken the spirit of contrition, to impart higher vitality to the soul, —in fine, to open up a channel of delightful communion between man and God. These broad facts of history are not to be swept away by the feeble scoffs of scepticism and unbelief.

18. If such a power be not in Nature nor in law, then, if it is to be found at all, it must be

found in God. But humanity needs a mediator.
How is he to be found in God? Who shall
ascend to Heaven to bring Him down from
thence? Who shall descend into the depths of
the infinite essence to bring Him up, in a full
disclosure of the purpose of the Godhead,
speaking in self-sacrificing love to man? A
higher revelation of divine perfection than any
that Creation affords is needed ; a new principle
is brought into the divine administration—a
power which, preserving intact the principles of
moral law, will change the precept of that law
in its demands upon the sinner, and require him
not to *act*, but to *believe* in order that he may
act. Where can the power be found which can
effect such a change in the mutual relations of
God and man?

19. With whom is the reconciling power to
begin? In man himself? The enmity in man
forbids the supposition. The whole experience
of human life on this earth proves that it never
has so originated. The nature of the finite
being excludes the supposition that it ever can
do so. God alone can bridge over the distance
between sinful Humanity and Himself.

20. Nor can this reconciliation be brought
about by a display of *divine wrath*. Does
anger in the parent generate filial love and

obedience in the child? Does severity in the prince foster loyalty in the subject? Does penal infliction on the part of the sovereign awaken gratitude in the criminal? No more can the outpouring of divine wrath secure the reconciliation of the sinner. He cannot confide or delight in a God speaking to him in vengeance, and in the stern severity of outraged law.

21. Nor can reconciliation be effected by a display of *authority*. Authoritative demands only produce fear and dread, or create enmity. If these demands have been already disregarded, the reiteration of them will not restore concord. That which did not prevent the sin will not raise the sinner. Neither will indulgence to the disobedient effect a reconciliation: it will only feed and foster selfishness.

22. Self-sacrifice, then, is the grand necessity of well-being to fallen man. And self-sacrifice can only come from the promptings of a generous heart. High attainment is possible to finite beings only through self-sacrifice. It is only by illustrious actions that a noble nature can rest in self-repose. The true reward of a noble life is the possession of the self-denying spirit. But, in order to the awakening of this spirit in fallen man, a manifestation of divine self-sacrifice on his behalf is necessary. It is only by such

an act that God can speak with elevating power to the fallen human spirit.

23. Eternal Love, spontaneously moved from its own inner depths in compassion for suffering humanity, sent forth His well-beloved Son that He might ally Himself with humanity and become its Emmanuel, displaying the infinite grace and perfection of the divine character—the Lamb of God, bearing away the sin of the world—and thus convincing it of its enmity to Himself. And man, displaying his hatred to God by nailing His Son to the accursed tree—an object of scorn and contempt to the world—did not understand that, in the profound mysteries of redemption, this very treatment of the Son enabled the Father to "lay on Him the iniquity of us all." But the same Eternal Love raised Him to the throne of the universe, invested Him with universal power and authority, that He might carry out the work of mediation and reconcile God and man.

24. The Godhead thus gave to the universe such a manifestation of its illimitable goodness and mercy as introduced a new power into the divine administration, fitted in its very nature to rescue man from sin, and to raise him to God. In entire consistency with all the perfections of His character and His hatred of sin, God can

now come to the sinner with the terms of reconciliation. "Mine anger is turned away." And
in so coming, God proves to the world that
there is nothing in Himself to make the sinner
afraid, but everything to encourage him and
calm his fears.

25. When, therefore, the hour had come for
the crisis of the stupendous conflict between
enmity in its fiercest and most intensified form,
and the perfection of obedience in the gentlest
act of self-sacrifice, the Son, in profound sympathy with a suffering race, and on behalf of
mankind, drank the full cup of divine wrath.
Thus was given the answer of the Godhead in
its most solemn utterance. He takes upon
Himself all the immeasurable consequences of
creating finite beings with free wills, in that
tremendous encounter of rebel enmity with
self-sacrificing devotedness; and, in doing so,
shows to the world the impossibility of leaving
sin unpunished. And thus He achieves all that
is fitted to break for ever the spell of the sinner's
delusion, and to destroy the charm of selfishness.
He bears, as only the Son of God could bear,
the full outburst of the rage of the Prince of
Evil. He supplicates forgiveness for His im-
placable foes; commends His spirit to His
loving Father; dies by the hand of "him who

had the power of death;" and pays the ransom of human salvation.

26. From the cross, then, goes forth to the universe the most august and solemn proclamation, "Be ye holy, for I am holy." In this, the most momentous event of time, the Godhead confronted all the consequences of creating finite free agency; displayed all the incomprehensible mystery of free will; realized all the mystery of suffering, in the glory of a self-sacrificial death. Before the gaze of the universe, the "Christ is made perfect through suffering." The Son, the special object of the Father's love, realizes the hiding of the Father's face, and cries aloud, "Eli, Eli, Lama Sabachthani!" The full mystery of atonement, veiled from mortal knowledge in time, will be comprehended by the redeemed above in the perfection of their immortality in eternity.

27. The sinner, by the eye of faith contemplating the event of Calvary, comprehends with the heart the truth there revealed. He ceases to dread God; comes to Him in filial love; and is no longer the victim of his own guilty conscience and corrupt heart. He believes that the living Father, self-moved in the spontaneous benignity of His heart towards mankind, has sent forth the Son of His love to lift human

nature into oneness with His own divinity, so that He might, in the stead of sinners, bear the full weight of God's displeasure, and introduce a new principle into the divine government—a reconciling principle—an instrumentality fitted to remove the guilt of sin from the conscience, and fill the soul with love to God. Must not the believer of these beneficent and elevating truths be brought into a new relation with God —the relation of reconciliation ?

28. The man who thus believes cannot remain longer in dread of God, or tremble under the apprehension of divine wrath. Nor can he desire that self should any longer occupy the throne of his heart. Neither can he doubt the purpose of Him who sits on the throne of the universe to reconcile all things to Himself ; nor refuse to co-operate with Him in the accomplishment of his own and the world's salvation.

29. Love is the reconciler. Love holds souls in concord and co-operation. Love is the cementing power of spiritual life and intercourse. But it must be intelligent love, covering nothing, concealing nothing. If love be self-sacrificing, adapting itself to the circumstances of the sinner, it must be sovereign. It must sway, control, and overrule all things for

the accomplishment of its own supreme end. It must reconcile all things in the creation of God, in the divine administration, and in the heart, the intellect, and the life of man.

30. Christ is our substitute. He has taken our place in that He took our nature. His life, His death, His resurrection and ascension, all are ours.

31. Christ has expiated our guilt. He has purged Humanity of self, and redeemed it from error and suffering, from death, from eternal ruin.

32. Christ is our propitiation. He has reconciled God to man, and man to God. He has restored man to God by renewing humanity and quickening it with the divine life. He has dowered humanity with the love of God, and caused God to delight in humanity as He beholds man renewed and restored.

33. Christ is our sacrifice. He has done all this for us. His self-denial in bearing the contradiction of sinners against Himself, submitting to temptation, enduring the conflict with Satan and the hiding of His Father's face, dying on the cross : was all for us.

34. Christ is our vicarious sacrifice. He bore all for us, to bring us to God by bringing God down to us. His death was not simply the death of a martyr testifying to the truth for

which He had lived. It was not merely the
sinking of human nature under the overwhelm-
ing load of the sins and suffering of our race.
It was the voluntary yielding up of Himself to
the powers of darkness in conformity with His
Father's will. It is a mirror in which the sinner
may behold his fixed .enmity to the divine
nature. And it opened up a medium for the
Father to exhibit the intense desire of His
heart, the self-sacrificing devotedness of His
purpose, and the awful limit to which he would
reach in creating the power that works human
salvation.

35. Christ is our atonement—the reconciliation in Himself of the divine administration
with the life of faith in the believing soul. In
Him the two natures are blended in one
personal life. In the divine administration the
law no longer demands punishment, but belief
in the divine mercy.

36. Christ is our salvation. The believer
in Jesus becomes of one spirit, mind, and life
with God's own Son. Thus it is that man is
reconciled to God, and God to man. In the
completed salvation in Heaven, man will be
perfected in the life of eternal love and joy.

IV.

THE UNPARDONABLE SIN.

CHAPTER IV.

THE UNPARDONABLE SIN.

1. SYMPATHY with truth is necessary to a comprehensive understanding of it. Even a dim discernment of the deep things of God can be reached only by simple-minded and believing inquiry, not into human systems, but into the principles of divine revelation. As the underlying principle of all Scripture truth is the disclosure of the self-sacrificing love of God, we must carefully keep this truth in view if we are to arrive at a correct conception of the divine purpose. No adequate conception can otherwise be formed of God's design in manifesting Himself to man.

2. Now, the enmity of the rebellious heart of man may be so inveterate, that no display of divine self-sacrifice on his behalf will induce him to regard that gracious display otherwise than as a design to enslave him.

3. If such a display of the Divine self-sacrifice as that given on Calvary was necessary to slay the enmity of the carnal mind to God, that

E

enmity must be a tremendous reality — the highest conceivable form of rebelliousness against the infinite Father. Its intensity surpasses man's own comprehension ; its insidious devices are unknown even to itself. The heart of man cannot conceive its manifold workings in withstanding the striving of the Spirit, or the restless efforts of the human intellect to corrupt and pervert the Gospel.

4. The two mightiest powers of earth—the political and the ecclesiastical—combined to destroy the Saviour Himself. Imperialism exerted its fiercest energy to destroy His Church. Heresy, in a thousand forms, has laboured, and does still labour, to corrupt His truth.

5. In view of this we perceive the amazing grace of God in bringing the conviction of His saving truth into the human understanding. The mission of the Son is the great miracle of the universe. But even this amazing wonder may seem to be surpassed when the work of the Spirit will be manifested in all its fullness. How very little we know of the long-suffering of the Spirit, in His gracious operations quickening the soul with the divine life, and carrying on the work of sanctification through His own immediate indwelling !

6. The necessity for this amazing long-suffering is grounded in the free will of man—the underlying principle of all God's dealings with him. So sacred is this free agency in the view of God, that all the manifestations of the divine purpose, and especially that of the divine self-sacrifice, are framed to meet its conditions. No violence can be done to the free will, no interference with it is permitted ; no ignoring of it can enter into any of God's dealings with man. Rather than that, God will Himself submit to self-sacrifice and will carry it to its utmost limits.

7. Why else are given to the human spirit "the gifts of the Holy Ghost," of "the good word of God," of "the powers of the world to come?" And why suffer it, notwithstanding those gifts, to fall away from the divine life? Is God, then, trifling with the soul's eternal interests? Is He displaying indifference to its salvation? None will dare to make so blasphemous an assertion. The *sacredness of the sinner's free will*, in his acceptance or refusal of the quickening divine grace, supplies the explanation. Hence springs the long-suffering of the Divine Spirit. In this aspect of God's dealings with man is exhibited the most astonishing display of the divine love and wisdom. There is

here found ample scope for grace to reign in righteousness for the unfolding of the most delicate relations in the accomplishment of ultimate divine results.

8. For, the bringing into clearest light of the inveterate enmity of the carnal mind to God, through the display of the divine long-suffering, opens up to view the awful depth of *possibilities* of abuse in the free will, and of the boundlessness of the self-sacrificing love of God. It is not in the evolution of the material universe, nor in the development of sentient being, but in the manifestations of the spiritual sphere, that we must look for the exhibition of self-sacrificing love. And the final exhibition may be in connection with the awful sin which the Saviour Himself pronounced unpardonable.

9. Now this unpardonableness does certainly not lie in any defect in the great atonement. The atonement was made, not only for *sinners*, but for *sin*. Its purpose was the reconciliation of sinners to God. And it is fully adequate for the salvation of all sinners.

10. Neither is the unpardonableness due to failure in the strivings of the Divine Spirit. The Spirit is the agent of human regeneration, which is effected in opposition to the sinner's own inclinations and desires. Regeneration is

wrought in the sinner by the spirit leading him to embrace the dispositions and desires of God as his own. But the change in the sinner is accomplished in strict accordance with, and in the full and unfettered exercise of, the powers and principles of his own free agency. In turning from the bondage of self to the freedom of Christ, the sinner, although acting in opposition to selfishness, acts in perfect accord with the powers or principles of his own spiritual being. He acts thus because he is influenced by the spirit of God.

11. Nor is the unpardonableness of sin due to any short-coming in the divine self-sacrificing love. This love is of the inmost essence of the divine nature. It can neither be limited nor exhausted in its desires or its efforts. It is as boundless and eternal as the Infinite God Himself. It is in the very nature of self-sacrificing love to do all that is possible for the accomplishment of its own ends. No limits can be set to its operation.

12. The unpardonableness, then, of this sin cannot be due to any defect in the atonement; for defect in the atonement would nullify its worth. Neither is it attributable to any failure in the strivings of the Holy Spirit; for such failure would neutralize it wholly. There can

be no defect nor deficiency in the highest and most perfect of all God's works. Nor, again, can the unpardonableness be owing to any short-coming in God's self-sacrificing love; for any such indifference would be fatal to the very existence of that love.

13. The unpardonableness of the sin lies, and only can lie, in the nature of the sin itself. This supreme sin differs in its very nature from all other sins that men commit. Its heinousness lies in quenching the operations of the Divine Spirit, striving with the sinner to bring him to a consciousness of the divine life. By this operation it is that the Spirit effects regeneration in the soul. The Spirit, in its enlightening grace, awakens in the sinner better and holier thoughts, feelings, and desires; but the sinner resists and grieves the Spirit, and so renders it an absolute impossibility for him to receive the forgiveness of this sin. The forgiveness is, *in fact*, the realization of the divine life in the soul. But the sinner wilfully puts away from him the life of God, and deliberately chooses to continue in a state of spiritual death.

14. While this condition is maintained, forgiveness is, in the very nature of things, impossible; for the sinner's pardon, being realized in the consciousness of the divine life in the

soul, in the enjoyment of reconciliation with God, and delight in doing His will, can never be known by him who resists the Spirit.

15. The forgiveness of sin, whilst the sinner continues to resist the Spirit, would involve contradiction. It would be the declaration of a pardon which is not real—a mockery on the part of God. It would be the existence of two opposite conditions of consciousness at the same moment—a condition of love to God, while the subject of this love was cherishing enmity in his heart — the consciousness of spiritual life, while the subject of it is under the power of spiritual death.

16. Forgiveness lies in the regeneration of the soul itself—in the revolutionizing of the disposition and will. The spirit of self-sacrifice is sub stituted for the dominancy of selfishness. The consciousness of this change is the realization of forgiveness by the sinner.

17. While the sinner resists the regenerating operation of the Spirit, and quenches the risings in his soul of the new unselfish disposition, he cannot by any possibility realize the life of God within him. He stands consciously unpardoned and condemned.

18. Does all this render the *after*-repentance of the sinner a blank impossibility? This might

readily be supposed, were there no self-sacrificing love in God. But if the self-sacrificing love of God embraces all mankind; if the atonement was made for all sin; if the Divine Spirit is grieved at the sinner's resistance and does not abandon him but with reluctance; may He not at an after-period return again, and in other circumstances, under different conditions, effect the sinner's repentance? Christ enjoined forgiveness not once, nor seven times, but to seventy times seven; and His Spirit will not be less forgiving than He has enjoined it on His disciples to be. If the sin against the Holy Ghost be rendered possible only through the striving of the Spirit Himself, may not the repentance of even the most heinous sinner be regarded as an after-triumph of God's long suffering grace, that will thrill the heart of the entire universe? If the greater the sin that is forgiven, the purer is the consciousness of the forgiven one, the more fervent his love, the deeper his devotion, the loftier his aims, will not self-sacrificing love do all within the vast compass of its power to lead even *such* a sinner to repentance?

19. Justice reigns in all God's dealings with His creatures. But as mercy has been raised above, although not at the expense of, justice,

may not the repentance of even the chief of sinners—the most obstinate rebel against grace —be the crowning act in man's redemption, the most stupendous display of self-sacrificing love ? There is no unwillingness in the Spirit of all grace to use all means to recover even the chief of sinners from destruction. Self-sacrificing grace comes in the form of bleeding love to win sinners to reconciliation ; and whilst realizing in the keenest anguish of His soul the enmity of the carnal mind against God, He exclaims, " Father, forgive them, for they know not what they do ! " Is there anything too hard for such love ? The very chief of sinners has been made the chief of saints on earth, for the very purpose that God might show forth in him the long-suffering of His grace. " To whom much is forgiven, the same loveth much." The pro- founder the depth of sin out of which the sinner is raised, the more glorious is the work of his salvation. This is the underlying fact in the experience of the great apostle of the Gentiles. And there may be in the distant vista of future ages visions of ever-brightening glory—visions disclosing in fuller measure a loftier power— the highest wonders of self-sacrificing love ; wonders which will delight the souls of angels and beatified spirits, as they learn more and more of the achievements of redeeming grace. This earth is the sphere of selfishness, of enmity and revenge, where it is felt to be hard to forgive, to love enemies, to bless them that curse, to do good to them that hate, and pray for them that despitefully use and persecute us. But in the loftier realms of being it will not be so. We shall learn to become like, and to imitate, our Father in heaven; and so to become perfect even as He is perfect.

V.

THE ELECTION OF GRACE.

CHAPTER V.

THE ELECTION OF GRACE.

1. THE perverting power of human prejudice has in none of its misconceptions of revealed truth been more apparent than in connection with the doctrine of the election of grace. The Jews clung to an election of mere divine favouritism. Their cherished notion was that God had chosen them to be His peculiar people. But in cherishing this false conception they excluded themselves from the election of grace.

2. The same perversion of the doctrine appeared early in the Christian church, and has more or less been cherished since by the various sects of Christendom. The idea of his being the special favourite of a partial God is still ardently cherished by many a self-deceiver.

3. There is a divine election, but not of favouritism. It is only by grace. It is an election, not of a few, but of countless myriads of the saved, innumerable as the sands by the sea-shore, or as the stars of heaven, transcending all human arithmetic.

4. The conception of an election of grace is the grandest thought which the finite mind can form of the action of the infinite mind. For, in this election, the infinite imparts Himself to the finite being in the fulness of the divine life, for the enjoyment of mutual fellowship throughout eternity. God and man mutually enter into endearing and enduring relations.

5. The election of grace includes all those of mankind who have yielded themselves up to, and have been transformed by, the gracious love of the Father, descending into the soul through the self-sacrifice of the Son. And the love of the Father through the Son is apprehended by the sinner through the quickening of the Divine Spirit.

6. This process is the inevitable condition of the divine power possessing itself of the fallen human nature. The necessity is grounded in the antagonism of the selfish heart to the divine will. Selfishness naturally hates all generosity and self-sacrifice. Humanity, while unperverted, is receptive and plastic to the indwelling of the Divine Spirit. But the selfish spirit is antagonistic to it. When the antagonism is overcome, the spirit becomes " poor," or emptied of self-will. Such spirits are loyally submissive to the reign of grace, and, therefore, " theirs is the kingdom of heaven."

7. This descent of the love of God into the heart of fallen man illustrates the more clearly its infinite depth and tenderness. It shows, at the same time, that there is in fallen humanity the possibility of the grandest display of God's gracious love.

8. In this possibility lies the mystery of the fall. The divine love embraced Humanity in creating man in the image of God. The act was in harmony with the perfection of Creation ; and was a manifestation of the supremacy of man over the lower creation. But in order that man might be raised into the realization of the indwelling of God, the infinite force of self-sacrificing love must be exhibited to the universe. The fall of Israel subserves "the fulness of the Gentiles."

9. The elect of grace stand to God in the nearest and most endearing relationship of being. They are the subjects of the Father's tenderest love, imparted to them in the grandest possible manner, and accomplishing in them its grandest and most glorious results.

10. But beyond man's original creation in God's image, regeneration raises the elect of grace above other finite existences, by quickening within them the highest possible conditions of the divine life. Nothing comes in between

them and the tenderest love of God. It holds
them in its divine embrace ; it pledges itself to
do for them whatsoever is possible for them in
their capabilities, and its own most gracious
outgoings. Whilst here the heirs of God are
made lower than their ministering angels, who are
" sent forth to minister to them who shall be
heirs of salvation." But this is only their temporary, not their permanent condition. When
they shall appear with Christ in His glory, and
shall reign with Him, *they* too shall be raised
far above all principalities and powers, thrones,
and dominions. They will enjoy the full parti-
cipation of the divine nature and life. They
will be the children of God, the brethren of
Christ, presented by the Spirit of God "fault-
less in the presence of His glory with exceeding
joy."

11. Amidst the innumerable and varied conditions of finite intelligence which may exist in
the universe, *they* will sustain the closest relation to the Father. The work of grace within
them draws them by the strongest cords,
quickens them with the divinest life, and de-
velopes in their experience the consciousness of
the most enduring fellowship with God. To
gain this end required the self-sacrifice, not
alone of the Son, but also of the Divine Spirit.

12. The elect are brought into this close relation to God by the most wonderful means and methods. Magnificent as is the work of Creation, it pales in splendour before the work of regenerating grace. To bring sinners into the election of grace, the Godhead travailed in the greatness of Its almighty strength. The mightiest oper ations of the divine power, the most amazing act of self-sacrifice in the outgoings of eternal love, were necessary to bring the rebellious back to their allegiance. So surpassing in its glory is it, that it absorbs the study of the heavenly intelligences. "Which things the angels desire to look into."

13. The new relationship is one of communicated spiritual vitality. In this earthly state it is apprehended through belief in Christ, and realized in the fellowship with the Divine Spirit. The believer grows in "meetness for the inheritance of the saints in light." The Church on earth is the training school for the Church in heaven.

14. There the elect of grace occupy the most conspicuous position in the universe : but not merely for their own enjoyment. A pure spirit can only find its enjoyment in employment worthy of its nature. The exaltation of the elect to the highest relation with the Godhead

F

makes them fitted for the most exalted employ-
ment. If the Godhead has engaged in its
loftiest undertaking for, and in, the elect, it must
be a fitting and worthy end. God does nothing
that does not become Himself. The wondrous
manifestations of divine grace were not accomplished solely for the sake of the saints themselves. Their rescue from the fall, their deliverance from sin, their elevation to the highest
rank of being, is a work which does not termi-
nate in itself. The elevation of "the heirs of
God" to the loftiest condition of being, so that
they may present to higher intelligences the
fullest revelation of God's grace, *must* be de-
signed in order that they shall shew forth in its
purest radiance that divine glory. These will
be the perpetual study of all heaven's intelligences. The self-sacrificing love of the Godhead
will, in them, be so conspicuously displayed, that
they will be the constant wonder and admiration
of the angels who once had been their ministering spirits. The end for which they are exalted,
and the manner of their exaltation, will awaken
in the breasts of angels the most adoring gratitude to God. These reflections of the divine
life in its purest radiance and highest glory will
cause the innumerable unfallen spirits to rejoice
and exult in God's mighty work of raising His

human children to such a pre-eminence of rank and dignity. And the saints in glory will be employed in such a manner as will be at once suitable to their illustrious condition and rank, and will especially exhibit the amazing nature of the self-sacrificing love that has exalted them so highly.

15. But the nearest fellowship with the God-head is possible only to spirits which bear the deepest consciousness of the divine life in the performance of the divine will through eternity. The employment of the elect in heaven will be such as will give to the intelligent universe a revelation of the Godhead unsurpassed in the history of creation. Their identification with their Lord in glory, in his final reign; their obligations to, and sympathy with, His self-sacrificing work on earth; their qualifications for, and delight in, self-sacrificing love for their Redeemer and Deliverer; will engage them to carry on its further displays into the eternity to come.

16. What may be the character of the employ-ment of the glorified in heaven is to us on earth unknown. We have only the feeblest indications, and the faintest hints in the Bible. The saints are to judge the angels; the suffer-ings of the present state are not worthy to be

compared with the glory which is to be revealed; and the creation which is now "made
subject to vanity," is waiting in earnest expecta-
tion for the manifestation of the sons of God.
They reign with Christ, and being the most
illustratious exemplifications of the divine self-
sacrifice, they will doubtless be the heralds of
the same divine grace to those who may still
be strangers to it. As the sun is the grandest
and most conspicuous object in the solar
system; as the milky-way is the brightest
cluster in the celestial horizon; even so are the
elect in the sphere of grace. The song of
victory they sing is one that cannot be learned
by other intelligences. The heavenly hosts
join joyfully in the chorus, "Great and marvellous are Thy works, Lord God Almighty, just
and true are Thy ways, Thou King of saints!
Who shall not fear Thee, O Lord, and glorify
Thy name; for Thou only art holy." But they
cannot sing the song of Moses and the Lamb.
They, never having struggled to rise superior to
sin, cannot occupy the place of the Redeemer.
The saints in glory are for ever separated from
all other intelligences by their consciousness of
their once being sinners, and of having been
saved from sin by the self-sacrifice of God's own
Son.

17. The elect, in their glorified state, give to the universe a full and complete revelation of the mystery of the creation of free will. The mystery is one which at present we cannot fathom, but still must believe. The opposition of wills has caused tremendous evil on this earth, not to speak of other spheres of existence. It may have been necessary to the fuller development and higher completion of the finite being. But we may rest in the assurance, that when the Godhead shall fully disclose the mystery, its creation will be seen to be in complete harmony with His infinitely blessed character.

18. The existence of suffering is inseparable from the abuse of free will, and the woes of earth offer an appalling spectacle to the thoughtful mind. And yet suffering is not a wholly unmitigated evil. Under its sharp discipline the loftiest heroism and the sublimest piety are matured. The Son of God Himself was made "perfect through suffering." And St Paul exultingly exclaims, that "the sufferings of the present state are not worthy to be compared with the glory that shall be revealed." When the mystery of suffering shall be disclosed, the greatest sufferers on earth will be the most joyful spirits of heaven, and the most fervent

feeling of gratitude in their hearts will be that, in the mystery of divine providence, they have been brought through suffering to realize the present unspeakable blessedness.

19. The mystery of dying into life will then be also made known. Though death in itself be the "last enemy," the brightest radiance and sweetest joy of the perfect state in heaven is secured to the saints through death. It may then be discovered that death was the necessary condition to entering into the consciousness of the higher life.

20. If, through the mystery of the creation of free will, the grandest achievements are wrought ; if, in connection with suffering, the sublimest life of man is secured ; if, through the dying of the Son of God, the salvation of a ruined race has been accomplished ; if, in the self-sacrifice of the Godhead, the foundation of the most illustrious condition of finite existence has been laid in time, to be fully realized in its highest perfection in eternity ; may we not rest in the assured confidence, that when these mysteries shall be developed to universal intelligence, the exulting hosts of heaven will burst forth in the lofty hymn, " Great and marvellous are Thy works, Lord God Almighty, just and true are all Thy ways, Thou King of saints !

Who shall not fear Thee, O Lord, and glorify Thy name, for Thou only art Holy!" All orders of being shall come and worship before Thee now that Thine infinitely wise and holy designs are all revealed!

21. In the struggles of life involved in the transition from self-will to self-sacrificing obedience, there is, doubtless, the richest and most important experience that can possibly be realized. Such an experience, in its length and breadth, height and depth, will afford comprehensive visions of being and life that will bring the soul into an identity with the divine object of the universe; justifying St Paul in his declaration of the perfect state as one in which the saved will " see as they are seen," and " know as they are known." The life of the redeemed will be so fully identified with the life of the Redeemer, the will of man will be so lost in its oneness with the will of God, that all selfishness will be annihilated.

22. The consummation of all will be FAITH REALIZED IN SIGHT. The kingdom is brought back to God the Father, and "GOD WILL BE ALL IN ALL."

APPENDIX.

ON THE REVISION OF CREEDS.

APPENDIX.

ON THE REVISION OF CREEDS.

1. THE one characteristic which distin -
guishes revelation from formularies of
human belief is that the former is from God,
whilst the latter are of man. The truth, coming
from God to man through inspiration, necessarily
comes under limiting conditions, but these leave
the infinite source ever unlimited. The limits
are in the *mode* of reading, not in the truth read.
A clear apprehension and conception of its
meaning can only be attained through careful
and prolonged study.

2. But formularies of human belief are but
the compilations of individuals of one age, or of
different periods of ecclesiastical history, endeav-
ouring, as best they can, to attain to a correct
apprehension of Scriptural truth. However fitted
they may be to give apt expression to the conceptions current in their age, they may yet not

be fitted for expressing those of after-generations.

3. To alter the inspired form of revelation
would, in any age, be presumptuous, and even
impious; but to adapt the formularies of one
generation to the more fully developed conceptions of a succeeding one is obviously quite
allowable.

4. For the men of any one age, however
learned, wise, and pious they may be, to stereo-
type their conceptions, and to bind the faith of
after-generations to their own special form of
expression, would be arrogance intolerable to
independent minds, and an unwarrantable interference with the freedom of Christian thought.

5. Happily, this was not the design of the
eminent men of former times who set themselves to the task of formulating the truths of
divine revelation. Their object was to raise a
bulwark around inspiration against the invasion
of deadly error.

6. Those framers had no intention of inter-
fering with Christian thought, or of imposing a
burden upon the enlightened intellect of after
ages. They were, in fact, both desirous and
careful to avoid the very appearance of doing
this. They did their allotted work as best they
could, laying after-generations under a deep

obligation to them for their pious labours in the cause of God's truths.

7. When errors arise within the Church, causing strife and division, the need for formularies is at once recognised. They become standards around which those who hold the same views of divine truth may rally for its defence. But it is not belief in formularies of faith, it is belief of the truth as it is in Jesus, that alone saves the soul. The immense importance of this difference cannot be too earnestly insisted upon. The Spirit of God, in building up souls to salvation, will make use of no other instrumentality than that which He Himself has revealed for this very purpose. And when He has revealed the very form of truth He will employ in this His own greatest work, we are not to suppose that He will sanction any form of merely human devising. This is a momentous difference, challenging the devout consideration of all Christians. Overlooking it may possibly be the explanation of the conflicting and disturbed state of the Churches at this present time.

8. The belief in formularies, however necessary it may be for effecting ecclesiastical ends, undeniably perpetuates divisions within the Church. The formularies tenaciously clung to in prefer-

ence to the simple truth as it is in Jesus, become idols of sectarianism, the worship of which seriously impedes the progress of Christianity. Formularies, being necessarily defective, cannot be of perpetual obligation. Their revision, as occasion may demand, should be undertaken in the spirit of brotherly love and of reverence for the truth. Their temporary character should be fully and frankly admitted.

9. The Church is bound to be progressive, advancing ever towards perfection. To aid its progression honest endeavours must be put forth by all sections of the Church to bring their various creeds and confessions as nearly into harmony as their increasing light will show them.

10. A Church which is adverse to the revision of its formularies must either regard them as already perfect and complete, or it must be indifferent to its own spiritual progress. It prefers the human forms of divine truth to those which the Holy Spirit has given. But even the Church which claims for itself infallibility has acknowledged the necessity of modifying its doctrinal standards at different points of history. A revision of formularies is doubtless attended with difficulties which may lead timid souls to shrink from the task when

it becomes a duty. But this does not justify their refusal. If a revision of the translation of the Old and New Testaments has been executed by authority, a revision of the formularies surely is justifiable. The work must not, however, be so executed as to cause still more divisions in the Church, and so endanger the advance of Christianity. It must be undertaken in a spirit of most tender fraternal kindness even to the weakest of the brethren.

11. The plea of absence of the men possessed of the needful learning, wisdom, and piety for the proper accomplishment of the revision is, in effect, a denial of the progressive character of the Christian Church. If creeds were formulated freely three centuries ago, it is certainly no compliment to the men of the present advanced age to put forth this plea for non-interference with its creeds.

The above may be summarised as follows :—

1. *Creeds, the nature of.*
A simple gathering-up of the received beliefs of a people at the time they were found.

2. *The object of Creeds.*
To provide a platform for organisation and work.

3. *Authority of Creeds.*

Merely human, not divine. The truth in them
is of God; the setting of that truth is of man.
The words in which the truth is set forth are
essential to the creed; and these being of man,
the creed is of man, not of God.

4. *Value of Creeds.*

The present and definite system of doctrine
given to the world is necessarily imperfect
through the limitations named; yet, in the main,
is good and worthy.

5. *Binding nature of Creeds.*

Obligatory on the conscience accepting it.
When it can be no longer held it ought to be
rejected.

6. *Permanence of Creeds.*

Men's opinions are ever passing through new
phases. This may necessitate a change in the
form of creeds.

7. *Present agitation.*

Much restlessness is apparent, but nothing
definite is proposed. Yet, in order to satisfy
those who are mentally troubled, something
should be done in the way of revision.

8. *What is possible?*

It would be rash to alter present creeds,

as many cling to them with devout tenacity, as being venerable and ecclesiastical historical documents. They should be allowed to remain untouched. But a shorter and simpler creed, suited to the requirements of the times, might be drawn up for popular and general use.

TURNBULL AND SPEARS, PRINTERS, EDINBURGH.

www.ingramcontent.com/pod-product-compliance
Lightning Source LLC
Chambersburg PA
CBHW021415090426
42742CB00009B/1150

9 7 8 3 3 3 7 3 6 7 9 5 4